# 95 Poems

*By E. E. Cummings*
*In Liveright paperback*

The Enormous Room
Etcetera
is 5
No Thanks
Selected Poems
Tulips & Chimneys
22 and 50 Poems
ViVa
XAIPE
1 X 1 [One Times One]

*In Liveright clothbound*

Complete Poems 1904–1962

# 95 Poems

# E. E. CUMMINGS

Edited, with an Afterword, by George James Firmage

LIBRARY
Archbishop Thomas J
Murphy High School
Northsound Association
for Catholic Education

Liveright

New York • London

First issued in Liveright paperback 2002
Copyright © 1958, 1971, 1972, 1986 by the E. E. Cummings Copyright Trust
Copyright © 1973, 2002 by George James Firmage

All rights reserved
Printed in the United States of America

For information about permission to reproduce selections from this book,
write to Permissions, Liveright Publishing Corporation, 500 Fifth Avenue,
New York, NY 10110

Library of Congress Cataloging-in-Publication Data

Cummings, E. E. (Edward Estlin), 1894–1962.
    95 poems / E. E. Cummings ; edited, with an afterword, by
George James Firmage.
        p. cm.
    **ISBN 0-87140-181-9**
    I. Title: Ninety-five poems. II. Firmage, George James. III.
Title.

PS3505.U334 A6 2002
811'.52—dc21

                                        2002072482

W. W. Norton & Company, Inc.
500 Fifth Avenue, New York, N.Y. 10110
www.wwnorton.com

W. W. Norton & Company Ltd.
Castle House, 75/76 Wells Street, London W1T 3QT


    5 6 7 8 9 0

# CONTENTS

# 95 Poems

to marion

|

l(a

le
af
fa

ll

s)
one
l

iness

## 2

to stand(alone)in some

autumnal afternoon:
breathing a fatal
stillness;while

enormous this how

patient creature(who's
never by never robbed of
day)puts always on by always

dream,is to

taste
not(beyond
death and

life)imaginable mysteries

now air is air and thing is thing:no bliss

of heavenly earth beguiles our spirits,whose
miraculously disenchanted eyes

live the magnificent honesty of space.

Mountains are mountains now;skies now are skies—
and such a sharpening freedom lifts our blood
as if whole supreme this complete doubtless

universe we'd(and we alone had)made

—yes;or as if our souls,awakened from
summer's green trance,would not adventure soon
a deeper magic:that white sleep wherein
all human curiosity we'll spend
(gladly,as lovers must)immortal and

the courage to receive time's mightiest dream

# 4

this man's heart

is true to his
earth;so
anyone's world
does

-n't interest him(by the

look
feel taste smell
& sound
of a silence who can

guess

ex-
actly
what life
will do)loves

nothing

as much as
how(first
the arri
-v-

in

-g)a snowflake twi-
sts
,on
its way to now

-here

# 5

crazy jay blue)
demon laughshriek
ing at me
your scorn of easily

hatred of timid
& loathing for(dull all
regular righteous
comfortable)unworlds

thief crook cynic
(swimfloatdrifting
fragment of heaven)
trickstervillain

raucous rogue &
vivid voltaire
you beautiful anarchist
(i salute thee

spirit colossal
(& daunted by always
nothing)you darling
diminutive person

jovial ego(&
mischievous tenderly
phoebeing alter)
clown of an angel

everywhere welcome
(but chiefly at home in
snowily nowheres
of winter his silence)

give me a trillionth
part of inquisitive
merrily humble
your livingest courage

because you take life in your stride(instead
of scheming how to beat the noblest game
a man can proudly lose,or playing dead
and hoping death himself will do the same

because you aren't afraid to kiss the dirt
(and consequently dare to climb the sky)
because a mind no other mind should try
to fool has always failed to fool your heart

but most(without the smallest doubt)because
no best is quite so good you don't conceive
a better;and because no evil is
so worse than worst you fall in hate with love

—human one mortally immortal i
can turn immense all time's because to why

dominic has

a doll wired
to the radiator of his
ZOOM DOOM

icecoalwood truck a

wistful little
clown
whom somebody buried

upsidedown in an ashbarrel so

of course dominic
took him
home

& mrs dominic washed his sweet

dirty
face & mended
his bright torn trousers(quite

as if he were really her &

she
but)& so
that

's how dominic has a doll

& every now & then my
wonderful
friend dominic depaola

gives me a most tremendous hug

knowing
i feel
that

we & worlds

are
less alive
than dolls &

dream

both eaching come ghostlike
(inch)wraithish(by inch)grin
ning heshaped two these(stroll
more slowly than trees)

dodreamingly phantoms
(exchanging)è vero
madonna(nudge whispershout)
laugh matching onceupons

each bothing(if)creep(by
if)timelessly foundlost
glad(children of)dirtpoor
(popes emperors)undeaths

through(slapsoothed by sundark)
brightshadowfully fountaining
man's thingfulest godtown
(kissed bigly by bells)

maggie and milly and molly and may
went down to the beach(to play one day)

and maggie discovered a shell that sang
so sweetly she couldn't remember her troubles,and

milly befriended a stranded star
whose rays five languid fingers were;

and molly was chased by a horrible thing
which raced sideways while blowing bubbles:and

may came home with a smooth round stone
as small as a world and as large as alone.

For whatever we lose(like a you or a me)
it's always ourselves we find in the sea

in time's a noble mercy of proportion
with generosities beyond believing
(though flesh and blood accuse him of coercion
or mind and soul convict him of deceiving)

whose ways are neither reasoned nor unreasoned,
his wisdom cancels conflict and agreement
—saharas have their centuries;ten thousand
of which are smaller than a rose's moment

there's time for laughing and there's time for crying—
for hoping for despair for peace for longing
—a time for growing and a time for dying:
a night for silence and a day for singing

but more than all(as all your more than eyes
tell me)there is a time for timelessness

# 12

lily has a rose
(i have none)
"don't cry dear violet
you may take mine"

"o how how how
could i ever wear it now
when the boy who gave it to
you is the tallest of the boys"

"he'll give me another
if i let him kiss me twice
but my lover has a brother
who is good and kind to all"

"o no no no
let the roses come and go
for kindness and goodness do
not make a fellow tall"

lily has a rose
no rose i've
and losing's less than winning(but
love is more than love)

# 13

So shy shy shy(and with a
look the very boldest man
can scarcely dare to meet no matter

how he'll try to try)

So wrong(wrong wrong)and with a
smile at which the rightest man
remembers there is such a thing

as spring and wonders why

So gay gay gay and with a
wisdom not the wisest man
will partly understand(although

the wisest man am i)

So young young young and with a
something makes the oldest man
(whoever he may be)the only

man who'll never die

but also dying

(as well as
to cry and sing,
my love

and wonder)is something

you have and i
've been
doing as long as to

(yes)forget(and longer

dear)our
birth's the because of a
why but our doom is

to grow(remember

this my sweet)not
only
wherever the sun and the stars and

the

moon
are we're;but
also

nowhere

# 15

on littlest this
the of twig three
souls sit
round with cold

three(huddling a-
gainst one immense
deep hell
-o of keen

moon)dream unthings
silent three like
your my
life and our

# 16

in time of daffodils(who know
the goal of living is to grow)
forgetting why,remember how

in time of lilacs who proclaim
the aim of waking is to dream,
remember so(forgetting seem)

in time of roses(who amaze
our now and here with paradise)
forgetting if,remember yes

in time of all sweet things beyond
whatever mind may comprehend,
remember seek(forgetting find)

and in a mystery to be
(when time from time shall set us free)
forgetting me,remember me

for prodigal read generous
—for youth read age—
read for sheer wonder mere surprise
(then turn the page)

contentment read for ecstasy
—for poem prose—
caution for curiosity
(and close your eyes)

once White&Gold

daisy in the Dust
(trite now and old)

lie we so must

most lily brief

(rose here&gone)
flesh all is If

all blood And When

un(bee)mo

vi
n(in)g
are(th
e)you(o
nly)

asl(rose)eep

# 20

off a pane)the
(dropp
ingspinson
his

back mad)fly(ly
who
all at)stops
(once

# 2 1

joys faces friends

feet terrors fate
hands silence eyes
love laughter death

(dreams hopes despairs)

Once
       happened
nowhere else
imagine
          Now

rapidly this

(a
   forest has slowly
Murdered the House)
hole swallows it
               self

while nobody

(and stars moon
sun fall rise come
go rain snow)

remembers

# 22

why from this her and him
did you and did i climb
(crazily kissing)till

into themselves we fell—

how have all time and space
bowed to immortal us
if in one little bed

she and he lie(undead)

# 23

albutnotquitemost

lost(in this br
am
bliest tangle of hi
llside)a

few dim tombstones

try to re(still u
ntumbled but slant
ing drun
kenly)mind

me of noone i ever &

someone(the others have
long ago laid
them)i never(selves
any than

every more silent

ly)heard(& how
look at it blue is the
high is
the deep is the far o my

darling)of(down

# 24

dim
i
nu
tiv

e this park is e
mpty(everyb
ody's elsewher
e except me 6 e

nglish sparrow
s)a
utumn & t
he rai

n
th
e
raintherain

# 25

that melancholy

fellow'll play
his handorgan
until you say

"i want a fortune"

.At which(smiling)he stops:
& pick
ing up a magical stick
t,a,p,s

this dingy cage:then with a ghost

's rainfaint windthin
voice-which-is
no-voice sobcries

"paw?lee"

—whereupon out(SlO
wLy)steps(to
mount the wand)a by no
means almost

white morethanPerson;who

(riding through space
to diminutive this
opened drawer)tweak

S with his brutebeak

one fatal faded(pinkish or
yellowish maybe)piece
of pitiful paper—
but now,as Mr bowing Cockatoo

proffers the meaning of the stars

14th st dis(because my tears
are full of eyes)appears.   Because
only the truest things always

are true because they can't be true

# 26

round a so moon could dream(i sus

pect)only god himself & as
loveless some world not any un

god manufacture might but man

kind yet in park this grim most(these

one who are)lovers cling & kiss
neither beholding a nor seen

by some that bum who's every one

# 27

jack's white horse(up

high in
the night
at the end
of doubleyou

4th)reminds me

in spite of his buggy of
lady godiva
& that(for no reason at
all)reminds

me the

cheerfulest goddamned
sonofabitch
i ever met
or hope to meet in

the course of a shall we say somewhat

diversified
(putting
it
quietly)

life was a blindman

Property of
Northbound Association
for Catholic Education

# 28

as joe gould says in

his terrifyingly hu
man man
ner the only reason every wo
man

should

go to college is so
that she never can(kno
wledge is po
wer)say o

if i

'd
OH
n
lygawntueco

llege

ev erythingex Cept:

that
's what she's
got

—ex

cept what?
why
,what it

Takes.   now

you know(just as
well as i
do)what

it takes;& i don't mean It—

&
i don't
mean any

thing real

Ly what
;or ev
erythi

ng which.   but,

som
e
th

ing:Who

# 30

what Got him was Noth

ing & nothing's exAct
ly what any
one Living(or some
body Dead
like
even a Poet)could
hardly express what
i Mean is
what knocked him over Wasn't
(for instance)the Knowing your

whole(yes god

damned)life is a Flop or even
to
Feel how
Everything(dreamed
& hoped &
prayed for
months & weeks & days & years
& nights &
forever)is Less Than
Nothing(which would have been

Something)what got him was nothing

a he as o
ld as who stag
geri
ng up some streetfu

l of peopl
e lurche
s viv
idly

from ti(& d
esperate
ly)m
e to ti

me shru
gg
ing as if to say b
ut for chreyesake how ca

n
i s
ell drunk if i
be pencils

# 32

who(at

her nons-
elf
's unself too
-thf-
ully lee
-r-

ing)can this plati

-num fl-
oozey
begin to(a
-lm-
ost)imagi
-n-

e she is

33

a gr

eyhaire
d(m
utteri
ng)bab
yfa

ced

dr(lun
g)u
(ing)
nk g

RowL

(eyeaintu)
s
(hfraiduh

nOHw

u
n)

!

## ADHUC SUB JUDICE LIS

when mack smacked phyllis on the snout

frank sank him with an uppercut
but everybody(i believe)

else thought lucinda looked like steve

"so you're hunting for ann well i'm looking for will"
"did you look for him down by the old swimminghole"
"i'd be worse than a fool to have never looked there"
"and you couldn't well miss willy's carroty hair"

"it seems like i just heard your annabel screech
have you hunted her round by the rasberrypatch"
"i have hunted her low i have hunted her high
and that pretty pink pinafore'd knock out your eye"

"well maybe she's up to some tricks with my bill
as long as there's haymows you never can tell"
"as long as there's ladies my annie is one
nor she wouldn't be seen with the likes of your son"

"and who but your daughter i'm asking yes who
but that sly little bitch could have showed billy how"
"your bastard boy must have learned what he knows
from his slut of a mother i rather suppose"

"will's dad never gave me one cent in his life
but he fell for a whore when he married his wife
and here is a riddle for you red says
it aint his daughter her father lays"

"black hell upon you and all filthy men
come annabel darling come annie come ann"
"she's coming right now in the rasberrypatch
and 'twas me that she asked would it hurt too much

and 'twas me that looked up at my willy and you
in the newmown hay and he telling you no"
"then look you down through the old swimminghole
there'll be slime in his eyes and a stone on his soul"

# 36

yes but even

4 or(&
h
ow)dinary
a

meri

can b
usiness soca
lled me
n dis

cussing "parity" in l'hô

tel nor
man(rue d
e l'échelle)
die can't

quite poison God's sunlight

# 37

handsome and clever and he went cruising
into a crazy dream
two were a hundred million whos
(while only himself was him)

two were the cleanest keenest bravest
killers you'd care to see
(while a stuttering ghost that maybe had shaved
three times in its life made three)

brawny and brainy they sing and they whistle
(now here is a job to be done)
while a wisp of why as thick as my fist
stuck in the throat of one

two came hurrying home to the dearest
little women alive
(but jim stood still for a thousand years
and then lay down with a smile)

# 38

s.ti:rst;hiso,nce;ma:n

c
ollapse
d

.i:ns;unli,gh;t:

"ah
gwonyuhdoanfool
me"

toitselfw.hispering

# 39

## THANKSGIVING (1956)

a monstering horror swallows
this unworld me by you
as the god of our fathers' fathers bows
to a which that walks like a who

but the voice-with-a-smile of democracy
announces night & day
"all poor little peoples that want to be free
just trust in the u s a"

suddenly uprose hungary
and she gave a terrible cry
"no slave's unlife shall murder me
for i will freely die"

she cried so high thermopylae
heard her and marathon
and all prehuman history
and finally The UN

"be quiet little hungary
and do as you are bid
a good kind bear is angary
we fear for the quo pro quid"

uncle sam shrugs his pretty
pink shoulders you know how
and he twitches a liberal titty
and lisps "i'm busy right now"

so rah-rah-rah democracy
let's all be as thankful as hell
and bury the statue of liberty
(because it begins to smell)

# 40

silence

.is
a
looking

bird:the

turn
ing;edge,of
life

(inquiry before snow

# 4 |

Beautiful

is the
unmea
ning
of(sil

ently)fal

ling(e
ver
yw
here)s

Now

# 42

from spiralling ecstatically this

proud nowhere of earth's most prodigious night
blossoms a newborn babe:around him,eyes
—gifted with every keener appetite
than mere unmiracle can quite appease—
humbly in their imagined bodies kneel
(over time space doom dream while floats the whole

perhapsless mystery of paradise)

mind without soul may blast some universe
to might have been,and stop ten thousand stars
but not one heartbeat of this child;nor shall
even prevail a million questionings
against the silence of his mother's smile

—whose only secret all creation sings

# 43

who(is?are)who

(two faces at a dark
window)this father and his
child are watching snowflakes
(falling & falling & falling)

eyes eyes

looking(alw
ays)while
earth and sky grow
one with won

der until(see

the)with the
bigger much than biggest
(little is)now(dancing yes for)white
ly(joy!joy!joy)and whiteliest all

wonderings are silence is becom

ing each
truebeautifully
more-than-thing
(& falling &)

EverychildfatheringOne

# 44

—laughing to find
anyone's blind
(like me like you)
except in snow—

a whom we make
(of grin for smile
whose head's his face
with stones for eyes

for mind with none)
boy after girl
each brings a world
to build our clown

—shouting to see
what no mind knows
a mindless he
begins to guess

what no tongue tells
(such as ourselves)
begins to sing
an only grin—

dancing to feel
nots are their whys
stones become eyes
locks open keys

haven't is have
doubt and believe
(like me like you)
vanish in so

—laughing to find
a noone's more
by far than you're
alive or i'm—

crying to lose
(as down someone
who's we ungrows)
a dream in the rain

# 45

i love you much(most beautiful darling)

more than anyone on the earth and i
like you better than everything in the sky

—sunlight and singing welcome your coming

although winter may be everywhere
with such a silence and such a darkness
noone can quite begin to guess

(except my life)the true time of year—

and if what calls itself a world should have
the luck to hear such singing(or glimpse such
sunlight as will leap higher than high
through gayer than gayest someone's heart at your each

nearerness)everyone certainly would(my
most beautiful darling)believe in nothing but love

# 46

never could anyone
who simply lives to die
dream that your valentine
makes happier me than i

but always everything
which only dies to grow
can guess and as for spring
she'll be the first to know

# 47

out of night's almosT Floats a colour(in

-to day's bloodlight climbs the onlying
world)
        whose
silence are cries
poems children dreams &

through slowquickly opening ifless

this irre-
VocA
-ble flame

is
   lives
        breath
              es(over-

ing
    un
-derfully & a-
rounding
          death)

L

o
v

e

# 48

someone i am wandering a town(if its
houses turning into themselves grow

silent upon new perfectly blue)

i am any(while around him streets
taking moment off by moment day
thankfully become each other)one who

feels a world crylaughingly float away

leaving just this strolling ghostly doll
of an almost vanished me(for whom
the departure of everything real is the
arrival of everything true)and i'm

no(if deeply less conceivable than
birth or death or even than breathing shall

blossom a first star)one

# 49

noone and a star stand,am to am

(life to life;breathing to breathing
flaming dream to dreaming flame)

united by perfect nothing:

millionary wherewhens distant,as
reckoned by the unimmortal mind,
these immeasurable mysteries
(human one;and one celestial)stand

soul to soul:freedom to freedom

till her utmost secrecies and his
(dreaming flame by flaming dream)
merge—at not imaginable which

instant born,a(who is neither each
both and)Self adventures deathlessness

# 50

!

o(rounD)moon,how
do
you(rouNd
er
than roUnd)float;
who
lly &(rOunder than)
go
:ldenly(Round
est)

?

# 51

f

  eeble a blu
r of cr
umbli
ng m

oo

  n(
poor shadoweaten
was
of is and un of

so

  )h
   ang
   s
   from

  thea lmo st mor ning

# 52

why

do the
fingers

of the lit
tle once beau
tiful la

dy(sitting sew
ing at an o
pen window this
fine morning)fly

instead of dancing
are they possibly
afraid that life is
running away from
them(i wonder)or

isn't she a
ware that life(who
never grows old)
is always beau

tiful and
that nobod
y beauti

ful ev
er hur

ries

# 53

n

ot eth
eold almos
tladyf eebly
hurl ing
cr u

mb

son ebyo
neatt wothre
efourfi ve&six
engli shsp
arr ow

s

# 54

ardensteil-henarub-izabeth)

this noN
allgotupfittokill
She with the
& how

p-e-r-f-e-c-t-l-y-d-e-a-d

Unvoice(which frightenS
a noisy most
park's
least timorous pigeons)squ

-I-

nts(while showe
ring cigaretteash O
ver that scre
Amingfeeblyoff

s,p;r:i;n,g

# 55

you no

tice
nobod
y wants

Less(not to men

tion least)& i
ob
serve no

body wants Most

(not
putting it mildly
much)

may

be be
cause
ever

ybody

wants more
(& more &
still More)what the

hell are we all morticians?

# 56

home means that
when the certainly
roof leaks it
's our(home

means if any moon
or possibly
sun shines they are
our also my

darling)but should some im
probably
unworld crash
to 1

nonillion(& so)nothings
each(let's
kiss)means
home

# 57

old age sticks
up Keep
Off
signs)&

youth yanks them
down(old
age
cries No

Tres)&(pas)
youth laughs
(sing
old age

scolds Forbid
den Stop
Must
n't Don't

&)youth goes
right on
gr
owing old

# 58

a total stranger one black day
knocked living the hell out of me—

who found forgiveness hard because
my(as it happened)self he was

—but now that fiend and i are such
immortal friends the other's each

# 59

when any mortal(even the most odd)

can justify the ways of man to God
i'll think it strange that normal mortals can

not justify the ways of God to man

# 60

dive for dreams
or a slogan may topple you
(trees are their roots
and wind is wind)

trust your heart
if the seas catch fire
(and live by love
though the stars walk backward)

honour the past
but welcome the future
(and dance your death
away at this wedding)

never mind a world
with its villains or heroes
(for god likes girls
and tomorrow and the earth)

61

Young m
oon:be kind to olde

r this
m

ost ol
d than(a

sleep)whom and tipto
e t

hrough
his dream;dancin

g you
Star

# 62

your birthday comes to tell me this

—each luckiest of lucky days
i've loved,shall love,do love you,was

and will be and my birthday is

# 63

precisely as unbig a why as i'm
(almost too small for death's because to find)
may,given perfect mercy,live a dream
larger than alive any star goes round

—a dream sans meaning(or whatever kills)
a giving who(no taking simply which)
a marvel every breathing creature feels
(but none can think)a learning under teach—

precisely as unbig as i'm a why
(almost too small for dying's huge because)
given much mercy more than even the
mercy of perfect sunlight after days

of dark,will climb;will blossom:will sing(like
april's own april and awake's awake)

# 64

out of the lie of no
rises a truth of yes
(only herself and who
illimitably is)

making fools understand
(like wintry me)that not
all matterings of mind
equal one violet

# 65

first robin the;
you say something
(for only me)
and gone is who.

since becomes why:
old turns to young
(winter goodbye)
april hello,

# 66

"but why should"

the
greatest
of

living magicians(whom

you and i
some
times call

april)must often

have
wondered
"most

people be quite

so(when flowers)in
credibly
(always are beautiful)

ugly"

# 67

this little huge

-eyed per-
son(nea
-rly burs-

ting with the

in
-expressib-
le

num

-berlessn-
ess of her
selves)can't

u

-nderstan-
d my o
-nl-

y me

# 68

the(oo)is

lOOk
(aliv
e)e
yes

are(chIld)and

wh(g
o
ne)
o

w(A)a(M)s

# 69

over us if(as what was dusk becomes

darkness)innumerably singular
strictly immeasurable nowhere flames
—its farthest silence nearer than each our

heartbeat—believe that love(and only love)

comprehends huger easily beyonds
than timelessly alive all glories we've
agreed with nothing deeper than our minds

to call the stars.   And(darling)never fear:

love,when such marvels vanish,will include
—there by arriving magically here—
an everywhere which you've and i've agreed
and we've(with one last more than kiss)to call

most the amazing miracle of all

# 70

whatever's merely wilful,
and not miraculous
(be never it so skilful)
must wither fail and cease
—but better than to grow
beauty knows no

their goal(in calm and fury:
through joy and anguish)who've
made her,outglory glory
the little while they live—
unless by your thinking
forever's long

let beauty touch a blunder
(called life)we die to breathe,
itself becomes her wonder
—and wonderful is death;
but more,the older he's
the younger she's

# 71

stand with your lover on the ending earth—

and while a(huge which by which huger than
huge)whoing sea leaps to greenly hurl snow

suppose we could not love,dear;imagine

ourselves like living neither nor dead these
(or many thousand hearts which don't and dream
or many million minds which sleep and move)
blind sands,at pitiless the mercy of

time time time time time

—how fortunate are you and i,whose home
is timelessness:we who have wandered down
from fragrant mountains of eternal now

to frolic in such mysteries as birth
and death a day(or maybe even less)

# 72

i shall imagine life
is not worth dying,if
(and when)roses complain
their beauties are in vain

but though mankind persuades
itself that every weed's
a rose,roses(you feel
certain)will only smile

# 73

let's,from some loud unworld's most rightful wrong

climbing,my love(till mountains speak the truth)
enter a cloverish silence of thrushsong

(and more than every miracle's to breathe)

wounded us will becauseless ultimate
earth accept and primeval whyless sky;
healing our by immeasurable night

spirits and with illimitable day

(shrived of that nonexistence millions call
life,you and i may reverently share
the blessed eachness of all beautiful
selves wholly which and innocently are)

seeming's enough for slaves of space and time
—ours is the now and here of freedom.   Come

# 74

sentinel robins two
guard me and you
and little house this our
from hate from fear

a which of slim of blue
of here will who
straight up into the where
so safe we are

# 75

(hills chime with thrush)

A
hummingbird princess
FlOaTs
doll-angel-life
from

Bet:To;Bouncing,Bet

the
ruby&emerald zigging
HE
of a zagflash king
poUnc

es buzzsqueaking th

ey
tangle in twitter
y t
wofroing chino
ise

r(!)i(?)e(.)s

# 76

these from my mother's greatgrandmother's rosebush white

roses are probably the least probable roses
of her improbable world and without any doubt
of impossible ours
                              —God's heaven perhaps comprises
poems(my mother's greatgrandmother surely would know)
of purest poem and glories of sheerest glory
a little more always less believably so
than(how should even omnipotent He feel sorry
while these were blossoming)roses which really are dreams
of roses—
                    "and who" i asked my love "could begin
to imagine quite such eagerly innocent whoms
of merciful sweetness except Himself?"
                                                        —"noone
unless it's a smiling" she told me "someone"(and smiled)

"who holds Himself as the little white rose of a child"

# 77

i am a little church(no great cathedral)
far from the splendor and squalor of hurrying cities
—i do not worry if briefer days grow briefest,
i am not sorry when sun and rain make april

my life is the life of the reaper and the sower;
my prayers are prayers of earth's own clumsily striving
(finding and losing and laughing and crying)children
whose any sadness or joy is my grief or my gladness

around me surges a miracle of unceasing
birth and glory and death and resurrection:
over my sleeping self float flaming symbols
of hope,and i wake to a perfect patience of mountains

i am a little church(far from the frantic
world with its rapture and anguish)at peace with nature
—i do not worry if longer nights grow longest;
i am not sorry when silence becomes singing

winter by spring,i lift my diminutive spire to
merciful Him Whose only now is forever:
standing erect in the deathless truth of His presence
(welcoming humbly His light and proudly His darkness)

# 78

all nearness pauses,while a star can grow

all distance breathes a final dream of bells;
perfectly outlined against afterglow
are all amazing the and peaceful hills

(not where not here but neither's blue most both)

and history immeasurably is
wealthier by a single sweet day's death:
as not imagined secrecies comprise

goldenly huge whole the upfloating moon.

Time's a strange fellow;
                    more he gives than takes
(and he takes all)nor any marvel finds
quite disappearance but some keener makes
losing,gaining
                    —love! if a world ends

more than all worlds begin to(see?)begin

# 79

whippoorwill this

moonday into
(big with unthings)

tosses hello


whirling whose rhyme

(spilling his rings)
threeing alive

pasture and hills

# 80

if the Lovestar grows most big

a voice comes out of some dreaming tree
(and how i'll stand more still than still)
and what he'll sing and sing to me

and while this dream is climbing sky
(until his voice is more than bird)
and when no am was ever as i

then that Star goes under the earth

here's s

omething round(& so
mething lost)& som
ething like
a mind with
out a body(turn
ing silently to a
lmost)dis
appearing
how patiently be

coming some(&

merciful
ly which is
every)un(star
rain snow moon
dream wing tree
leaf bird
sun
& singing &)
thing found

one old blue wheel in a pasture

# 82

now comes the good rain farmers pray for(and
no sharp shrill shower bouncing up off
burned earth but a blind blissfully seething
gift wandering deeply through godthanking ground)

bluest whos of this snowy head we call
old frank go bluer still as(shifting his life
from which to which)he reaches the barn's immense
doorway and halts propped on a pitchfork(breathing)

lovers like rej and lena smile(while looming
darkly a kindness of fragrance opens around
them)and whisper their joy under entirely the coming
quitenotimaginable silenceofsound

(here is that rain awaited by leaves with all
their trees and by forests with all their mountains)

# 83

perished have safe small
facts of hilltop
(barn house wellsweep
forest & clearing)

gone are enormous
near far silent
truths of mountain
(strolling is there here

everywhere fairyair
feelable heavenless
warm sweet mistfully
whispering rainlife)

infinite also
ourselves exist sans
shallbe or was
(laws clocks fears hopes

beliefs compulsions
doubts & corners)
worlds are to dream now
dreams are to breathe

# 84

how generous is that himself the sun

—arriving truly,faithfully who goes
(never a moment ceasing to begin
the mystery of day for someone's eyes)

with silver splendors past conceiving who

comforts his children,if he disappears;
till of more much than dark most nowhere no
particle is not a universe—

but if,with goldenly his fathering

(as that himself out of all silence strolls)
nearness awakened,any bird should sing:
and our night's thousand million miracles

a million thousand hundred nothings seem
—we are himself's own self;his very him

# 85

here pasture ends—
this girl and boy
who're littler than
(day disappears)

their heartbeats dare
some upward world
of each more most
prodigious Selves

both now alive
creatures(bright if
by shadowy
if)swallowing

is everywhere
beginningless
a Magic of
green solitude

(go marvels come)
as littler much
than littlest they
adventure(wish

by terror)steep
not guessable
each infinite
Oblivions

found a by lost
child and a(float
through sleeping firsts
of wonder)child

unbreathingly
share(huge Perhaps
by hugest)dooms
of miracle

drift killed swim born
a dream and(through
stillness beyond
conceiving)dream

until No least
leaf almost stirs
as never(in
againless depths

of silence)and
forever touch
or until she
and he become

(on tiptoe at
the very quick
of nowhere)we
—While one thrush sings

# 86

this
forest pool
A so

of Black
er than est
if

Im
agines
more than life

must die to
merely
Know

# 87

now(more near ourselves than we)
is a bird singing in a tree,
who never sings the same thing twice
and still that singing's always his

eyes can feel but ears may see
there never lived a gayer he;
if earth and sky should break in two
he'd make them one(his song's so true)

who sings for us for you for me
for each leaf newer than can be:
and for his own(his love)his dear
he sings till everywhere is here

# 88

joyful your complete fearless and pure love
with one least ignorance may comprehend
more than shall ever provingly disprove
eithering vastnesses of orish mind

—nothing believable inhabits here:
overs of known descend through depths of guess,
shadows are substances and wings are birds;
unders of dream adventure truths of skies—

darling of darlings!by that miracle
which is the coming of pure joyful your
fearless and complete love,all safely small
big wickedly worlds of world disappear

all and(like any these my)words of words
turn to a silence who's the voice of voice

now what were motionless move(exists no

miracle mightier than this:to feel)
poor worlds must merely do,which then are done;
and whose last doing shall not quite undo
such first amazement as a leaf—here's one

more than each creature new(except your fear
to whom i give this little parasol,
so she may above people walk in the air
with almost breathing me)—look up:and we'll

(for what were less than dead)dance,i and you;
high(are become more than alive)above
anybody and fate and even Our
whisper it Selves but don't look down and to

-morrow and yesterday and everything except love

rosetree,rosetree
—you're a song to see:whose
all(you're a sight to sing)
poems are opening,
as if an earth was
playing at birthdays

each(a wish no
bigger than)in roguish
am of fragrance
dances a honeydunce;
whirling's a frantic
struts a pedantic

proud or humble,
equally they're welcome
—as if the humble proud
youngest bud testified
"giving(and giving
only)is living"

worlds of prose mind
utterly beyond is
brief that how infinite
(deeply immediate
fleet and profound this)
beautiful kindness

sweet such(past can's
every can't)immensest
mysteries contradict
a deathful realm of fact
—by their precision
evolving vision

dreamtree,truthtree
tree of jubilee:with
aeons of (trivial
merely)existence,all
when may not measure
a now of your treasure

blithe each shameless
gaiety of blossom
—blissfully nonchalant
wise and each ignorant
gladness—unteaches
what despair preaches

myriad wonder
people of a person;
joyful your any new
(every more only you)
most emanation
creates creation

lovetree!least the
rose alive must three,must
four and(to quite become
nothing)five times,proclaim
fate isn't fatal
—a heart her each petal

# 9 |

unlove's the heavenless hell and homeless home

of knowledgeable shadows(quick to seize
each nothing which all soulless wraiths proclaim
substance;all heartless spectres,happiness)

lovers alone wear sunlight.   The whole truth

not hid by matter;not by mind revealed
(more than all dying life,all living death)
and never which has been or will be told

sings only—and all lovers are the song.

Here(only here)is freedom:always here
no then of winter equals now of spring;
but april's day transcends november's year

(eternity being so sans until
twice i have lived forever in a smile)

# 92

i carry your heart with me(i carry it in
my heart)i am never without it(anywhere
i go you go,my dear;and whatever is done
by only me is your doing,my darling)
                                        i fear
no fate(for you are my fate,my sweet)i want
no world(for beautiful you are my world,my true)
and it's you are whatever a moon has always meant
and whatever a sun will always sing is you

here is the deepest secret nobody knows
(here is the root of the root and the bud of the bud
and the sky of the sky of a tree called life;which grows
higher than soul can hope or mind can hide)
and this is the wonder that's keeping the stars apart

i carry your heart(i carry it in my heart)

spring!may—
everywhere's here
(with a low high low
and the bird on the bough)
how?why
—we never we know
(so kiss me)shy sweet eagerly my
most dear

(die!live)
the new is the true
and to lose is to have
—we never we know—
brave!brave
(the earth and the sky
are one today)my very so gay
young love

why?how—
we never we know
(with a high low high
in the may in the spring)
live!die
(forever is now)
and dance you suddenly blossoming tree
—i'll sing

being to timelessness as it's to time,
love did no more begin than love will end;
where nothing is to breathe to stroll to swim
love is the air the ocean and the land

(do lovers suffer?all divinities
proudly descending put on deathful flesh:
are lovers glad?only their smallest joy's
a universe emerging from a wish)

love is the voice under all silences,
the hope which has no opposite in fear;
the strength so strong mere force is feebleness:
the truth more first than sun more last than star

—do lovers love?why then to heaven with hell.
Whatever sages say and fools,all's well

if up's the word;and a world grows greener
minute by second and most by more—
if death is the loser and life is the winner
(and beggars are rich but misers are poor)
—let's touch the sky:
                with a to and a fro
(and a here there where)and away we go

in even the laziest creature among us
a wisdom no knowledge can kill is astir—
now dull eyes are keen and now keen eyes are keener
(for young is the year,for young is the year)
—let's touch the sky:
                with a great(and a gay
and a steep)deep rush through amazing day

it's brains without hearts have set saint against sinner;
put gain over gladness and joy under care—
let's do as an earth which can never do wrong does
(minute by second and most by more)
—let's touch the sky:
                with a strange(and a true)
and a climbing fall into far near blue

if beggars are rich(and a robin will sing his
robin a song)but misers are poor—
let's love until noone could quite be(and young is
the year,dear)as living as i'm and as you're
—let's touch the sky:
                with a you and a me
and an every(who's any who's some)one who's we

# AFTERWORD

## by

## George James Firmage

The last volume of new poems to be published before Cummings's death was preceded, four years earlier, by *Poems 1923–1954*, the collected edition of his poetry up to 1950. The poet had originally entitled the book *Poems 1923–1950*, the dates representing the years of publication of the first and last books in the collection. However, the publishers, Harcourt, Brace and Company, made the final date of the title the year of the collection's publication. As Cummings told Robert Giroux, Harcourt's editor in chief, "if our non(even more than usual)hero signed a contract reading '1954',it's obvious that noone's at fault but himself."[1]

The publisher's successful promotion of *Poems 1923–1954*—the volume won the National Book Award's special citation in 1955 and went through three large printings of almost 30,000 copies in less than four years—led to their undertaking the publication of *95 Poems*. As issued in October 1958, it was a large "bookofpoems" by modern standards and intended, as its author told the present writer, to make "all those slim volumes look even slimmer."

The book's contents were arranged by the poet with his characteristic attention to detail. As he told Francis Steegmuller in a letter dated 5 March 1959, *95 Poems* represented "an obvious example of the seasonal metaphor—1,a falling leaf;41,snow;73,nature(wholeness innocence eachness beauty

---

1. Charles Norman, *The Magic-Maker: E. E. Cummings* (New York: The Macmillan Company, 1958), p. 382.

the transcending of time&space) awakened. 'Metaphor' of what? Perhaps of whatever one frequently meets via my old friend S. ForsterDamon's William Blake/His Philosophy And Symbols;e.g.(p 225)'They' the angels 'descend on the material side. . .and ascend on the spiritual;this is. . .a representation of the greatest Christian mystery,a state- ment of the secret which every mystic tries to tell."'[2]

The texts and settings of the poems in the present edition are based on the poet's complete typescript of the book in The Houghton Library, Harvard University.

---

2. *Selected Letters of E. E. Cummings* (New York: Harcourt, Brace and World, 1969), p. 261.

W '11

T 12200